SCIENCE KIDS

PLANT PATTERNS

Aaron Carr

MEDIA ENHANCED BOOK

www.av2books.com

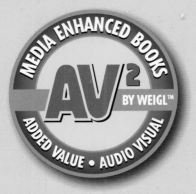

MEDIA ENHANCED BOOKS
AV²
BY WEIGL™
ADDED VALUE • AUDIO VISUAL

Go to **www.av2books.com**, and enter this book's unique code.

BOOK CODE

F550315

AV² by Weigl brings you media enhanced books that support active learning.

AV² provides enriched content that supplements and complements this book. Weigl's AV² books strive to create inspired learning and engage young minds in a total learning experience.

Your AV² Media Enhanced books come alive with...

Audio
Listen to sections of the book read aloud.

Video
Watch informative video clips.

Embedded Weblinks
Gain additional information for research.

Try This!
Complete activities and hands-on experiments.

Key Words
Study vocabulary, and complete a matching word activity.

Quizzes
Test your knowledge.

Slide Show
View images and captions, and prepare a presentation.

...and much, much more!

Published by AV² by Weigl
350 5ᵗʰ Avenue, 59ᵗʰ Floor New York, NY 10118
Website: www.av2books.com   www.weigl.com

Library of Congress Cataloging-in-Publication Data

Carr, Aaron.
 Plant Patterns / Aaron Carr.
    p. cm. -- (Science kids)
 ISBN 978-1-61690-946-8 (hardcover : alk. paper) -- ISBN 978-1-61913-038-8 (pbk) -- ISBN 978-1-61690-592-7 (online)
 1. Pattern perception--Juvenile literature. 2. Color in nature--Juvenile literature. I. Title.
 BF294.C37 2012
 152.14'23--dc23
                          2011023417

Printed in the United States of America in North Mankato, Minnesota
2 3 4 5 6 7 8 9 0 17 16 15 14 13

072013
WEP110613

Project Coordinator: Aaron Carr   Art Director: Terry Paulhus

Weigl acknowledges Getty Images, iStock, and Dreamstime as image suppliers for this title.

PLANT PATTERNS

CONTENTS

What pattern do you see?

A leaf has a pattern of lines.

What pattern does wood have?

5

What pattern do you see?

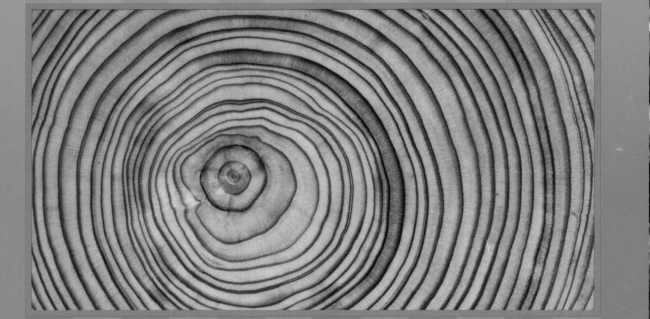

Wood has a pattern of round lines.

What pattern do flowers have?

What pattern do you see?

Flowers have a pattern of colors.

What pattern does a tulip have?

What pattern do you see?

These tulips have a pattern of red and yellow colors.

What pattern does this leaf have?

What pattern do you see?

Some leaves have a pattern of triangles along their edges.

What pattern do these plant leaves make?

What pattern do you see?

Some plant leaves make a spiral pattern.

What pattern does broccoli have?

What pattern do you see?

This broccoli has a pattern of bumps.

What pattern does a sunflower have?

What pattern do you see?

Sunflowers have a pattern of colorful bumps.

What patterns do pineapple leaves have?

What patterns do you see?

Pineapple leaves have patterns of lines, colors, and triangles.

CAN YOU FIND THESE PATTERNS?
Lines   Colors   Triangles   Bumps

23

WORD LIST

Research has shown that as much as 65 percent of all written material published in English is made up of 300 words. These 300 words cannot be taught using pictures or learned by sounding them out. They must be recognized by sight. This book contains 19 common sight words to help young readers improve their reading fluency and comprehension. This book also teaches young readers several important content words, such as proper nouns. These words are paired with pictures to aid in learning and improve understanding.

Sight Words		
a	has	their
along	have	these
and	lines	this
can	make	what
do	of	you
does	see	
find	some	

Page	Content Words First Appearance
4	pattern
5	leaf, wood
7	flowers
9	colors, tulip
13	edges, plants, triangles
15	broccoli, spiral
17	bumps, sunflower
19	pineapple